Praise for the Lesson Downton Abbey Book Series

Leadership Lessons From Downton Abbey

"This book is a great introduction to the world of leadership and management and offers a handy overview of key leadership principles and management strategies... I loved *Downton Abbey* so for me the book was a delight. It's practical and easy to read and makes sense of sometimes complex issues."

SaskBooks Reviews

"One of the things the book pulls nicely together after these four sections (leading yourself, leading employees, leading culture, leading with others) is what you refer to as effective leadership and the four critical areas—insight, self-discipline, courage and influence. Those things are transcendent whether we are in the earliest part of the 20th century or now in the earliest part of the 21st... It's a very interesting read."

John Gormley, Broadcaster, Lawyer, Author, Former Member of Parliament

Change Management Lessons From Downton Abbey

"Writers Jeanne Martinson and Laurelie Martinson have leveraged their interests in management, communications, leadership, and the popular British TV series *Downton Abbey* to inform business and organizational leaders... There's much interesting material here, for both leaders and laypeople."

SaskBooks Reviews

"Very interesting new book... In Season Two, (Downton Abbey) gets its first telephone. That was an amazing time in the earliest part of the 20th century for managing change. So much of our current rapid technological change is simply finding new tools or techniques to do what we already do. This was completely a new paradigm altogether."

John Gormley, Broadcaster, Lawyer, Author, Former Member of Parliament

LEADERSHIP LESSONS FROM DOWNTON ABBEY

by
Jeanne Martinson
Laurelie Martinson

A WOOD DRAGON BOOK

This book has not been approved, licensed, or sponsored by any entity or person involved in creating or producing the television series, **Downton Abbey.**

Leadership Lessons From Downton Abbey
By Jeanne Martinson and Laurelie Martinson

Copyright 2017 Jeanne Martinson and Laurelie Martinson

Published by:
Wood Dragon Books
P.O. Box 429
Mossbank, Saskatchewan
Canada
S0H3G0

Telephone +1.306.591.7993
www.wooddragonbooks.com

Cataloguing and Publication Data available from
Library and Archives Canada

ISBN: 9780995334281

Inside and cover art by *Laurelie Martinson*

Dedication

We all have people in our lives who
have taught us how to lead -
through triumph or disaster,
through kindness or cruelty,
through wisdom or folly.

This book is dedicated to the people
who taught us that
when it comes to leadership –
character counts.

Note from the Authors

As a consultant and manager who has spent more than 25 years helping and leading organizations, I have often observed a disconnection between leadership and management — where we spend our time visioning the future only to fail in the present. Our current culture is addicted to the new and bored with the old, but sometimes we can fix the problems of the present by applying some lessons from the past. Downton Abbey provides a wonderful analogy for discussing classic leadership and management tools in a new way.

Laurelie Martinson

The idea for this book came from a discussion about the many interesting leadership and management examples dramatized in the television series, *Downton Abbey*. The discussion grew and soon we were comparing the scenes in the drama set a century ago to leadership behaviour today.

Although this is my tenth book, it was definitely the most fun to write. Not only was researching *Downton Abbey* entertaining — but writing with my sister and long-time collaborator was as well.

Jeanne Martinson

Caveats

The authors recognize that employee rights and benefits enjoyed today were only in their infancy at the end of WWI. In many ways, the consequences of WWI pushed forward labour reforms such as pensions, reasonable hours of work and increased wage rates.

Pronouns correspond with the male and female leaders characterized in each chapter. Scenes described in the chapters do not necessarily appear in the chronological order portrayed in *Downton Abbey*.

Mrs. Hughes' skeleton key:

It unlocks the door to treasure — the store cupboard at Downton Abbey — the leadership insights and management strategies in this book.

Table of Contents

Introduction

ownton Abbey is an iconic British television series that captivated the world with its portrayal of the transition of family, society, and institutional life during the years immediately before and after World War I. The television series received BAFTAs, Emmys, Screen Actors Guild awards, Golden Globes, and holds the Guinness World Record as the Most Critically Acclaimed Television Show—all of which makes it Britain's most successful export in television history. Not only did *Downton Abbey* sweep away its viewers with dramatic characters, eye catching costumes and cinematography—it presented lessons that can be applied to our world today. Using the strengths and weaknesses demonstrated by the leaders in *Downton Abbey*, this book explores key leadership principles and management strategies.

British estates, as characterized by *Downton Abbey*, represented one of the largest business models of their time. These estates were multifaceted—ranging from agricultural production of crops and animals to supporting industries and services such as sawmills, repair shops, hospitals, and housing developments. Their structure influenced what would become our traditional, hierarchical, business model with executive, senior, and middle layers of management.

On the surface, *Downton Abbey* appears to be merely a story about a wealthy family with domestic servants and a grand house. But under the surface, we see the challenges of modernization faced by the leaders of this large scale interwoven enterprise. Through the illustration of *Downton Abbey*, we can explore the functions and the obligations of its executive and senior management and how their decisions drove the local economy and its corresponding culture. Regardless of whether a reader is familiar with the story of *Downton Abbey*, the lessons in this book provide practical advice to increase effectiveness as a leader, manager and boss.

Leader, Manager, Boss—it wasn't that long ago that these three terms meant the same thing. And for many employees in organizations today, they still do. My leader—is my manager—is my boss. Regardless of how senior the position a leader holds, if they have direct reports, they are de facto—a manager.

It is important that we understand how these terms have been refined over the last several decades.

Leadership and management are two separate functions. According to J. Kotter writing in the *Harvard Business Review*, management and leadership are separate, distinct and complimentary systems of action.[1] Leaders are focused on what the future can bring, including its possible opportunities, changes and distractions. It involves setting direction, aligning people and resources to that vision and motivating them to that end. Managers focus on the here and now, the current situation and the challenges faced in the moment. Management involves the tasks of planning and budgeting, organizing and staffing, controlling and problem solving. Leaders ask and answer the questions, what and why? Managers ask and answer the questions, who and how?

Organizations cannot succeed with leadership or management talent alone. As noted by J. Kotter, "While improving their ability to lead, companies should remember that strong leadership with weak management is not better, and is sometimes actually worse than the reverse."[2] Organizations need both leadership and management mindsets and functions within their ranks.

Leadership Lessons from Downton Abbey is neither a comprehensive volume of leadership theory nor is it an

academic guide on management. It is a lighthearted discussion of basic principles and strategies that lay the foundation for organizational success and career fulfillment.

Organizational Structure & Corresponding Roles

Executive Management
(Lord Grantham, Lady Grantham, Matthew Crawley, Lady Mary Crawley)

In the organization of Downton Abbey, the executive management team also happens to be a family. The television series begins with Lord Grantham being the sole owner and functioning CEO of the estate. Eventually, he shares ownership with his son-in-law, Matthew Crawley, who invests his own money to stabilize the finances of the estate. Upon Matthew's death, his wife, Lady Mary takes on the role of co-owner. Lady Grantham is part of the executive team as head of the household and leader of multiple community projects.

Lord Grantham
Matthew Crawley/Lady Mary Crawley

Man of Business	Agent	Butler
Mr. Murray	Mr. Jarvis/Mr. Branson	Mr. Carson

Man of Business

The Man of Business reports directly to executive management (Lord Grantham) and acts as an advisor in all legal and financial matters pertaining to the organization. He functions as a CFO and works from his London office.

Agent

The Agent oversees all tenancy contracts, businesses, and property on the land and estate. Reporting directly to executive management (Lord Grantham), he functions as a COO or General Manager.

Butler

The Butler is the most senior member of household staff, directly reporting to executive management (Lord Grantham). He is in charge of hiring, training, disciplining and firing male staff members, specifically under butlers, valets, footmen and hall boys. He is responsible for the prudent management of resources, security of the silver, and the inventory of the wine cellar.

Lady Grantham

Housekeeper	Cook	Hospital Administrator
Mrs. Hughes	Mrs. Patmore	Dr. Clarkson

Housekeeper

The Housekeeper is head of the domestic staff, reporting directly to executive management (Lady Grantham). She is in charge of hiring, training, disciplining, and firing female staff members, specifically ladies' maids and house maids. She is responsible for the maintenance and standards of household cleanliness, ordering of inventory and security of the store room, cleaning and inventory of all linen, and managing the household budget and accounts.

Cook

The Cook is in charge of the kitchen department and reports directly to executive management (Lady Grantham). She is in charge of hiring, training, disciplining, and firing of kitchen staff members, specifically assistant cooks, kitchen maids and scullery maids. She is responsible for maintaining the health of family, guests, and staff through nutritional menu design and preparation of delicious, visually appealing, gourmet meals.

Hospital Administrator

The Hospital Administrator reports directly to executive management (Lady Grantham). He manages the delivery of healthcare services to the village and the maintenance and functioning of the estate-funded hospital.

Senior Management
(Butler, Housekeeper, Cook, Agent)

The members of the senior management team report directly to executive management and have one or multiple direct reports. They oversee and manage their corresponding departments and functions and supervise the front line managers such as under butlers, head grooms, head gardeners, and assistant cooks.

Butler
Mr. Carson

Under Butlers	Valets	Footmen
Mr. Barrow	Mr. Bates/Mr. Molesley	Thomas/William/Alfred/James

Under Butlers

The Under Butlers report to senior management. They are responsible for the training and mentoring of footmen and junior male staff as well as tasks assigned by the senior management. They fill the position of butler when the butler is not present.

Valets

Reporting to senior management and the executive member to whom they are assigned, Valets are in charge of maintaining the wardrobe and attending to all manner of personal needs. They also provide companionship and security while travelling away from the estate.

Footmen

The Footmen report to the under butler and senior management. They are responsible for all manner of table service, opening and closing doors, delivery of messages and items, providing valet service to visitors, and any additional duties as required.

Housekeeper
Mrs. Hughes

Ladies' Maids
Miss O'Brien

House Maids
Gwen/Anna/Edna

Ladies' Maids

Reporting to senior management and the executive member to whom they are assigned, Ladies' Maids are in charge of maintaining the wardrobe and attending to all manner of personal needs. They also provide companionship and security while travelling away from the estate.

House Maids

House Maids report to senior management. They are responsible for the tasks and duties to maintain the cleanliness of the house with the exception of the kitchen department and staff bedrooms.

Cook
Mrs. Patmore

Assistant Cook
Daisy

Kitchen Maids
Daisy

Assistant Cook

The Assistant Cook reports to the Cook and is directly involved in the preparation and cooking of the meals including main courses, vegetables and desserts.
(Daisy)

Kitchen Maids

The Kitchen Maids report to the cook and assistant cook. They are responsible for the cleanliness of the kitchen department including the scullery and larder. They may be called upon to clean vegetables or do additional tasks as directed. (In absence of a scullery maid, a kitchen maid may also be required to start the fires in the bedrooms or in the stove/range.)
(Daisy)

Notes
1. Only the staff mentioned in the subsequent chapters are included in the organizational charts above.
2. Daisy and Thomas/Mr. Barrow are mentioned multiple times according to their changing roles.

Leading Yourself

Discerning Motivation
Humble Honesty
Career Fluidity
Protecting Legacy
Practicing Generosity

*"It will be
a huge wrench
for me to leave Downton."*

Mr. Carson

Chapter One
Discerning Motivation

ady Mary Crawley was engaged to Sir Richard Carlyle, a self-made millionaire who sought to run a household equal to the best houses in England. To this end, he invited Mr. Carson, the butler at Downton Abbey, to lead his staff and household at Haxby Hall. It would have meant an increase in salary, a full complement of staff of Mr. Carson's choosing, and the opportunity to continue to serve and protect Lady Mary who had a special place in his heart. Mr. Carson accepted the position but later discovered that Sir Richard intended to spy on Lady Mary. Mr. Carson withdrew his acceptance of the position as he considered Carlyle's actions to be unethical and he could not work for such a man.

Mr. Carson was torn between his loyalty to Lord Grantham and his years at Downton Abbey and his affection for Lady Mary and the increased opportunity offered at Haxby Hall. His situation illustrates how motivation may affect a leader's decision-making when faced with a new career opportunity.

Mr. Carson was torn between making a choice that would provide emotional satisfaction and financial benefit with one that was aligned with his personal values and legacy. He had spent his entire career at Downton Abbey, joining the staff as a junior footman for Lady Mary's grandfather. Leaving this workplace in the twilight of his career would have been a monumental change in his life and only his affection for Lady Mary would provide compensation for the loss of that legacy.

Leaders who do their job well are often headhunted with flattering offers and financial incentives. However, if a leader does not have the discernment to know their foundational values, they may be tempted to make a change that results in a lowering of their passion and a diminishing of their capacity to be a good leader.

Certainly there is nothing wrong with a leader taking a position that provides more money or perhaps promises less responsibilities or a lighter work schedule. The danger is taking a position for one of these reasons at the expense of intrinsic personal values.

Every leader must believe in what they are doing and why they are doing it. Values are personal and so is the manner in which an individual lives them. It is not necessary to have identical values to your employer; it is more important for a leader to discern what his own values are and decide how to live them.

In the *Journal of Business Ethics*, Posner and Schmidt found a clear relationship between awareness of personal values and job satisfaction and commitment.[3]

Here are their findings:

> Low clarity on personal values
> + low clarity on organizational values
> = Commitment Score of 4.90
>
> Low clarity on personal values
> + high clarity on organizational values
> = Commitment Score of 4.90
>
> High clarity on personal values
> + low clarity on organizational values
> = Commitment Score of 6.12
>
> High clarity on personal values
> + high clarity on organizational values
> = Commitment Score of 6.26

From this study, we see that people may be very clear about their organization's values and still not have job satisfaction or be highly committed to the organization. However, the people who understand their personal values, even if they cannot articulate their company's values, are more likely to remain and contribute.

Individuals who understand both their personal values and the organization's values are the most likely to have high job satisfaction, commitment, and engagement. It is essential for a leader to be aware of this dynamic, not only for their career path, but understanding the motivations of their team.

In conclusion, the more a leader knows himself, the more likely he will stay on a path of true career fulfillment.

"He threatened to expose my past,
to make me a laughing stock
in this house,
and in my vanity and pride,
I gave him what he wanted."

Mr. Carson

Chapter Two
Humble Honesty

rior to becoming a butler, Mr. Carson had the scandalous career of singing and dancing on the stage. With his partner, Charlie Grigg, he made up the duo called the 'Cheerful Charlies'. Mr. Carson left this career to go into service where he was very successful, moving from junior footman to the highest position in household management. During these same years, Charles Grigg fell into a life of deceit and petty crime. Discovering Mr. Carson's high position in a prominent household, Grigg used the threat of exposing their theatrical past to blackmail his ex-partner. Mr. Carson, in an effort to conceal his past, stole food, gave it to Grigg, and hid him in a vacant estate house.

Grigg, dissatisfied with Mr. Carson's response to his demands for money, went to Downton Abbey to reveal to Lord Grantham Mr. Carson's past in hopes of separating the Earl from some cash. The situation came to a head with Mr. Carson, Mr. Grigg, and Lord Grantham. Mr. Carson confessed to his employer his actions to bury his career history and conceal the movements of his blackmailer.

Like Mr. Carson, perhaps we have chapters in our past that we would rather not have out in the open or revealed to those in our workplace.

Lying in the workplace becomes more frequent. A 2017 survey from The Society of Human Resource Managers reported that 53% of the resumes and job applications received contained falsifications, such as misleading statements, fraudulent degrees, altered employment dates, inflated salary claims, inaccurate job descriptions, and falsified references. In another online survey of 18,000 respondents conducted by AOL Jobs, 26.5% of respondents said that they either have in the past or would consider lying on a resume.[5]

Certainly today, leaders may be tempted to use the excuse that "everyone else is doing it", but it is important to remember that as leaders our success is a result of the sum of all of our experiences, both positive and negative. We want to fully accept the truth and its consequence. The last thing we want is for our lack of acceptance of the past to cause us to make poor choices in the present.

If a leader upgrades past job titles, denies relationships with others, twists the reasons or circumstances for which they left a position, or elevates a current role to a more powerful one—they may excuse these falsehoods as trivial. Yet this dishonesty may be rooted in shame, a lack of self-acceptance, or a fear that judgment may thwart an opportunity.

Mr. Carson was concerned that his staff and employer would think less of him if his "Cheerful Charlie" past was revealed. What is ironic is that his reputation was harmed more by his lies and theft than his past life on the stage. If a leader suggests that he left a position on his own accord when in fact he was asked to leave for cause, the fact that he misrepresented his leaving will do more damage than if the initial circumstances were revealed.

In an effort to protect our reputation, we may destroy it.

*"I am having
my career backwards."*

Mr. Molesley

Chapter Three
Career Fluidity

M r. Molesley was recruited as butler/valet to serve Matthew Crawley (the future Earl of Grantham) and his mother at Crawley House. With the death of Matthew Crawley, Mr. Molesley's position in the household was re-evaluated. Not only were the services of valet no longer necessary, neither was the role of butler as Mrs. Crawley decided to live a quieter life with minimum household staff.

Mr. Molesley moved in with his father and began working in the village as a manual labourer. After a while, he was offered the role of footman at Downton Abbey. He was reluctant to accept the position because he considered it a fall in status after his previous position of butler/valet at Crawley House. Finally coming to terms with the fact that his career prospects in the village were bleak, Mr. Molesley accepted the position of footman. This lesser role at Downton Abbey allowed Mr. Molesley to take an interest in the education of the assistant cook, Daisy. Upon the departure of Miss Bunting (Daisy's tutor), Mr. Molesley stepped in as mentor, working with the local headmaster to arrange for Daisy to sit examinations. As a result of these interactions, the headmaster of the school recognized Mr. Molesley's education and talent and offered him a permanent leadership position as teacher at the school.

It is only through looking back could Mr. Molesley recognize the winding path he took to his leadership role within the educational system.

Sometimes leadership opportunities don't come with a title. Mr. Molesley functioned as a leader from start to finish in his mentorship of Daisy. He helped her with her homework, provided resources, took her to art galleries and museums when they were both working in London, requested her father-in-law to encourage her when she was about to abandon her studies, arranged for her examinations, and even coached her through sample examination papers.

Although Molesley was leading informally in Daisy's education, he only defined his degree of career success by his current job title of footman. This resulted in his feeling personally dissatisfied and defeated by his inability to progress in what he perceived to be his chosen field. However, Mr. Molesley's role as footman allowed him the time to mentor and teach Daisy. His reduced consequence actually led to the opportunity to become a teacher.

In today's world of downsizing and amalgamation, the organizational chart and corresponding titles have become a roulette wheel where the same people are moved to different departments with the same leaders but with different titles and job descriptions. Just when everyone settles in, a new CEO comes onboard and spins the wheel once again.

In many organizations today, there is no longer a clear hierarchy with discernable upward mobility. This traditional linear career path, where an individual is hired for a job and moves up to more well paid and responsible positions, is only one path present in today's workplace.

Researchers D. Foot, R. Venne and M.J. Driver describe two other career paths: spiral and transitory. On the spiral path, we move slowly up and then over and around, trading in our goals of authority and position for education, retraining and experiences. We might even have multiple types of jobs within one organization.

On the transitory career path, a leader would have multiple employers and multiple jobs over their lifetime, moving from different teams and projects in ways that are both lateral and upward. Any of these three career paths (linear, spiral, or transitory) can provide opportunities for leadership and career fulfillment.[7]

What defines a leader is whether or not they are leading—not what the title is on their business card.

"*Of course I am concerned, Carson,*
and you must help me.
You know how dear you are to me,
and if there are changes
that need to be made,
we mustn't be afraid to face them."

Lady Mary Crawley

Chapter Four
Protecting Legacy

t the end of his career, Mr. Carson began to have tremors in his right hand. He attempted to hide this fact from those he reported to and those who reported to him. When serving champagne at a family wedding, his tremor prevented him from filling the glasses and he cried out in frustration. This drew the attention of many and the very thing he was seeking to hide became public. As a result, Lady Mary and Lord Grantham were forced to act and make a decision for Mr. Carson that he should have made for himself. They chose to move him into semi-retirement with a pension and a senior consulting role in the organization. They hired Mr. Barrow to replace Mr. Carson. Although Mr. Barrow was not Mr. Carson's preferred choice of a replacement, his procrastination resulted in him having no influence on the decision.

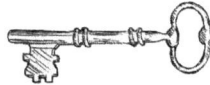

Mr. Carson knew his condition had finished the careers of both his father and grandfather. He knew that it was not a condition he would recover from. Had Mr. Carson accepted his changing ability, he would have been the one in charge of his workplace accommodation and choosing his replacement. By delaying action, Mr. Carson sacrificed the dignity of planned transition and instead became a pitiable creature in the eyes of others in his workplace.

We all come to the end of our careers at different times and for different reasons. Sometimes, we have achieved all we can achieve. Some, like Mr. Carson, are affected by illness or disability. Some choose to retire for increased time with family and grandchildren. Others leave due to overwhelming changes in technology and some from burnout. The essential key is accepting that, for whatever reason, we are no longer right for the role or the role is no longer right for us. One of Mr. Carson's highest values was dignity, yet he lost some of his own by not accepting and leading this transition.

Mr. Carson's denial put pressure on the organizational system; his peers felt obligated to cover his errors and his employees had to take on extra duties and responsibilities. Mr. Carson's denial left his employers in a position where they were forced to intervene and take the timing of his retirement and the choice of successor out of his hands.

It is important for leaders who care about a lasting legacy to consider the impact of their decisions — both in large ways and small. Mr. Carson did not have a wake-up call in time to transition with dignity and create a positive legacy, but some leaders do.

On April 13, 1888, Alfred Nobel picked up a French newspaper and was surprised by the headline erroneously proclaiming his passing. Disheartened, he continued to read the obituary item which began: "The merchant of death is dead". It continued: "Dr. Alfred Nobel, who became rich by finding ways to kill more people faster than ever before, died yesterday." Alfred Nobel was, of course, the inventor of dynamite.

Eight years later when Nobel did eventually die, his obituary read something quite different. He had reflected on how he wished to be remembered and decided to change his will and, in doing so, his legacy. When he died in 1896 at the age of 63, the world was shocked to hear that he had designated more than 90% of his immense wealth to the creation of a series of prizes to be conferred upon those who contribute the "greatest benefit on mankind" in areas such as chemistry, physics, literature, medicine, and peace. The first Nobel prizes were awarded in 1901 just prior to the societal changes that are described in Downton Abbey.

In Mr. Carson's case, his lack of action caused a negative effect on employees, peers, and employers and compromised the very legacy he was trying so hard to build and be remembered for. In Mr. Nobel's case, shoddy journalism provided him the wake-up call in time to make different decisions to leave a different legacy.

Being aware allows a leader to set their own alarm clock so they are not caught off guard making decisions that negatively affect how they are remembered.

"I have an idea that when you mentioned Mrs. Harding's connection with us, you were trying to catch her out. I don't like to see such things, Barrow, I don't care for a lack of generosity."

Lord Grantham

Chapter Five
Practicing Generosity

wen Harding was formerly a house maid at Downton Abbey who left service to become a secretary at a telephone company. After working in local government, she met and married her husband and they both became involved in a new university for women called Thorncroft. Gwen and her husband were invited to Downton Abbey to discuss the university with Lord Grantham's sister, Rosamund, who was a trustee.

Gwen's rise in status stirred jealousy within Mr. Barrow, the acting butler, and he took the opportunity to expose her past in an inappropriate manner during luncheon. Following the luncheon, the staff and family gathered downstairs in the servants' hall to further their visit with Gwen. Lord Grantham immediately took Mr. Barrow aside to address what he considered inappropriate behaviour.

When Mr. Carson returned, Mr. Barrow's role as interim butler ended and he thanked Lord Grantham, saying he had enjoyed his time as butler. Lord Grantham responded, "*I hope you've learned something from it. You see, Barrow, Carson is a kind man. Don't overlook that. It's why people are loyal to him,*" reminding Mr. Barrow of the previous negative feedback and encouraging him to be gracious and generous in any further leadership role.

Leaders need to allow people to leave their past in the past. No one will be loyal to a leader if they think that at any moment their past will be regurgitated in an attempt to diminish them in the eyes of others. Mr. Barrow's disclosure of Gwen's past role came from a jealous, small and ungenerous part of who he was. A leader should highlight the best of people, unless there is a reason for direct negative feedback — which should be given in private.

The challenge for Mr. Barrow was that Gwen's success felt unfair to him because he was struggling to move forward in his own career and he knew his positon of under butler at Downton Abbey would be eliminated upon the return of Mr. Carson. His frustration with his own circumstances justified, in his mind, his unkindness to Gwen.

But as a leader in the role of under butler, Mr. Barrow did not have the luxury of acting or communicating based only on his negative feelings. He was in the role of authority, mentor, and role model.

In today's society, social media and reality television have led people to believe that they can exist solely within the emotional aspect of their personality and that somehow emotional responses are now acceptable in the workplace. Certainly, our emotions are part of who we are and we have the choice as to how we express them. But we also have to live with the consequence of how we express them, even if the consequence is one of reprimand.

Barrow did not have to like Gwen as a person to act in a generous way. As the noted English writer Samuel Johnson said, "Kindness is in our power, even when fondness is not."[10]

A person with petty and emotional responses will be interpreted as a petty and emotional leader.

Along with Mr. Barrow's behaviour discussed in this chapter, it is important to note that generosity is not just a behavioral tool for the individual, but is a social value that can transform a workplace.

This is not a new idea. Emily Post, who wrote at the time of *Downton Abbey*, penned many books in an effort to bring what was considered to be the "civilized etiquette" of Europe to the new world.[11] Post's advice, penned a hundred years ago, is by no means antiquated, but is essential in the modern workplace. As she said, "Custom is a mutable thing; yet we readily recognize the permanence of certain social values. Graciousness and courtesy are never old-fashioned."

Leading Employees

Defined Roles
Strengthening Mentorship
Direct Communication
Direct Feedback
Maintaining Accountability
Taking Action

"No, I won't be coming.
If I came, they wouldn't have fun.
They'd spend the day
looking over their shoulder
... I'm their leader."

Mr. Carson

Chapter Six
Defined Roles

hile the family was away in Scotland, the Downton Abbey staff got wind of a community fair being hosted in the nearby town of Thirsk. In an effort to gain permission to attend, the staff suggested to Mr. Carson and Mrs. Hughes that they all go to the fair as one large group. The senior management team (Mrs. Hughes, Mrs. Patmore, Mr. Carson) discussed the proposed plan and agreed that they would let the staff attend. Mrs. Patmore was going to the fair on a first date with a gentleman and Mrs. Hughes was going to accompany her. Mrs. Hughes encouraged Mr. Carson to come to the fair because it would be fun. Mr. Carson refused, citing that it would not be appropriate for him, as leader, to attend the fair with his staff.

Mr. Carson's concern was that his staff would not enjoy themselves during their time away from work if they knew he was present. They would feel compelled to maintain the formal protocols that were required at Downton Abbey instead of being able to let their hair down.

The flattening of the organizational structure and the increase of socialization between employees at all levels has led to a blurring of behavioural norms that previously were identified clearly as either work norms or social norms.

In many of today's organizations, we have seen a reduction of hierarchy, an increase in self-directed work teams, a decrease in direct supervision, and creation of an egalitarian culture. The benefits of this model are increased creative work, cross functionality of tasks, and a more adaptive workforce. The challenge these changes present is that it is difficult for a leader to maintain the defined roles and their corresponding boundaries and to act with authority when he has been functioning with his subordinates as a peer. It is difficult for the leader to then direct and discipline an employee and it is equally difficult for that employee to acquiesce to the leader's request.

It is vital for a leader to manage the boundaries of the relationships in the workplace, not only with subordinates, but also with colleagues. If a leader's career goal is to move up the organization, he must be mindful that today's colleague might be tomorrow's superior or subordinate.

During the time of *Downton Abbey*, there was little to no socialization between employees and their colleagues, let alone employees and their leaders. If there were any company social events, they were usually limited to one or two a year such as a company Christmas party or a summer picnic. But even within these social environments, the role of the leader was still very evident. Often these events had a specific agenda that included the leaders of the organization addressing the attendees, followed by awards for years of service, and recognition of the success of the organization and those who were responsible highlighted.

Over the past several decades, the definition of the appropriate social interaction between levels of hierarchy has become diffused. Corporate volunteer projects that strengthen team cohesion no longer end at the place of activity, but extend to a wrap up party at a local pub. Company golf tournaments with alcohol readily available can quickly open up the opportunity for inappropriate language, humour, and behaviour.

With the advent of social media, social interaction boundaries have disintegrated. Everyone up and down the organizational chart wants to friend each other on Facebook, where they not only are informed of each other's social activities, but have a private window into each other's entire social experience. This informality encourages employees to post comments regarding leadership, coworkers' activities, organizational products and services, even company policy on social media platforms—often overlooking workplace boundaries and company brand.

So how do organizations stop employees from posting inappropriate comments on social media? Scott Monty, former Global Digital and Multimedia Communications Manager at Ford Motor Company, suggests, "the same way it can keep employees from doing stupid things on email and the phone. Give them guidelines and resources. Have an online communications policy that follows standard communication policies and trust them to do the right thing."[13]

Maintaining roles and accompanying boundaries may not be simple in today's world. But like all problems of this type, the strategy remains the same: create a policy, communicate the policy, communicate the consequences of not following the policy, and act decisively if the policy is violated.

"Mr. Carson
has been a kind
and wonderful teacher."

Alfred Nugent

Chapter Seven
Strengthening Mentorship

lfred Nugent joined the staff at Downton Abbey as a footman, although he was formally trained as a waiter in a hotel. Having never worked as a footman prior to his arrival, he appealed to Mr. Carson for instruction. Alfred was enthusiastic to learn new skills and to perform his tasks to the best of his ability and Mr. Carson mentored Alfred in the tasks of his new role. When Mr. Carson was instructing Alfred on spoons, Thomas, the other footman, overheard the learning session and commented, "You're taking a lot of trouble with young Alfred, Mr. Carson. I feel quite jealous." Thomas assumed that Mr. Carson was showing favouritism towards Alfred by mentoring him.

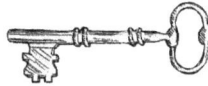

At the time of Downton Abbey, many crafts or trades were learned through mentorship, both by watching and following good examples and through direct training and apprenticeship. A good leader didn't expect someone to understand the entire job or be able to do the entire job perfectly without ongoing training or mentoring.

It is easy for a leader or manager to mentor those who are enthusiastic and likable. It is less easy to mentor those who seem disgruntled or not fully engaged in their role. However, without mentorship, these latter employees will be even less likely to be engaged and successful when they do not feel competent in their duties.

The leader may pick his most successful or senior staff member to train the new hire, but that might not be the best choice. If a leader does not take an active role in mentorship and leaves the training to other staff, they miss the opportunity to resolve poor performance as it arises. Although it takes time and effort, when a leader considers the cost of rework or mistakes an employee may make in the future, it is prudent to take charge of their development to ensure success.

Consider the four stops on the learning continuum — from not knowing to full competence and confidence:

1. There is considerable direction from the leader to the learner. If the learner has minimum knowledge of the task, he needs to be told what to do, how to do it, when and why. The leader decides and communicates direction. To not do so would leave the learner feeling unsupported.

2. Once the learner has basic knowledge and experience of the task, the leader then listens to the learner's input prior to making the decision.

3. As the competence and confidence of the learner grows, the leader moves into the role of coach where he helps clarify the decision before it is carried out.

4. Full delegation is when the employee is both competent and confident enough to make the decision completely on their own. To not delegate at this level of competency leaves the employee feeling micro-managed.[15]

Mr. Carson created a work environment open to mentorship. In an organization, the leader may have to articulate this open environment and communicate who mentors whom and how employees access mentorship.

Mentorship must be seen as fair and available to all—not as favouritism or an opportunity for one-on-one time with a superior to develop a more personal relationship. Mentorship time should be dedicated to actual skill development versus personal conversation or relationship building.

Golfing is not mentorship—unless you work at a golf course. Mentorship is when we talk about work while teaching and learning work skills, on work time. Managers who "mentor" employees while doing leisure activities and call it "mentorship' create confusion regarding the definition of mentorship. Whether the manager intended it or not, other employees may perceive such activities as favouritism.

A leader needs to be diligent regarding how they manage their mentorship processes to avoid misperceptions, both by the learner and other employees.

"It's not nothing, is it?"

Ms. Patmore

Chapter Eight
Direct Communication

aisy was a kitchen maid who had been working alongside the cook, Mrs. Patmore, for several years. As she advanced her skills, she became unhappy with her lot in life. She felt mistreated and taken advantage of. But rather than directly communicating with her manager and asking for promotion, Daisy used indirect communication and body language to express her discontent. From the heavy sighs over peeling potatoes to the slamming of pots and pans about the kitchen, Daisy communicated her unhappiness. In response to a direct question from Mrs. Patmore as to what was wrong, Daisy said nothing. To which Mrs. Patmore, who knew there was a problem and was growing frustrated with Daisy's behavior, responded, "It's not nothing, is it?"

After several months of this emotional behaviour, Daisy visited her father-in-law Mr. Mason, who recommended that she quit "sulking and answering back" and make her case for promotion to Mrs. Patmore. Daisy took Mr. Mason's advice and made her request in a direct and professional manner. Mrs. Patmore replied, "Why couldn't you have spoken of this sensibly the other night, instead of going off into a pet?" and promised to see if money could be found in the budget for her requested promotion.

Whether an employee is aware and attempting to deliberately influence others or is unaware and has a personal lack of control over their emotions, the effects of this kind of behaviour in the workplace are the same:

A leader may be tempted to fall into an unconscious codependent response and indulge the negative behaviour rather than intervene to address the behaviour.

Secondly, the inappropriate behaviour may create a work atmosphere that verges on hostile, and results in low productivity as employees work in an environment where the usual professional and positive responses are absent.

Thirdly, an emotionally charged workplace can quickly separate into factions where other employees commiserate and take sides in what is now a public discord.

In the situation above, Daisy was clearly aware of her communication strategy. Like Mrs. Patmore, in a similar situation, today's leader should call the employee in for a private conversation and ask them to articulate the issue at hand. If the employee decides not to reveal the issue, the leader must immediately communicate that the inappropriate behaviour must cease as it has become a performance problem.

It is the leader's responsibility to manage the emotional level and tone of the work space so that honest and direct conversation is the norm. In order to avoid problems as previously discussed, it is essential for the leader to define communication ground rules of appropriate emotional expression for incoming employees from their first day onward.

If a leader does not address this behaviour immediately, it allows all employees to believe that the behaviour is not only acceptable, but is a good strategy to achieve their desired outcome.

*"I hear you are becoming
mighty imperious in your manner
with the staff here,
Daisy in particular …
there's no need for rudeness.
So mind what I say."*

Dr. Clarkson

Chapter Nine
Direct Feedback

ord and Lady Grantham offer their personal home of Downton Abbey to be used as a convalescent hospital during World War I. After being discharged from the army, Thomas returned to Downton Abbey, not as a servant, but as a Sergeant in the Army Medical Core. He was promoted into management of the convalescent hospital, reporting directly to Doctor Clarkson. This position placed him in authority over the majority of the front line staff of the household. He used this opportunity to intimidate and publicly criticize Daisy (a kitchen maid at this time). News of his behaviour reached the ears of his superior, Major Clarkson, MD who addressed it immediately.

Managers generally dislike giving negative feedback. That is only human nature. However, by giving confusing feedback or no feedback at all, the manager sets up the employee for failure and the organization for possible legal issues because the employee has not been given an opportunity to truly learn how they could improve.

Positive feedback is given to increase the self-esteem of the employee and to ensure that the employee continues behaviour that the leader has identified as positive. Negative feedback is given to an employee to coach the employee to begin a new behaviour that he or she is not currently exhibiting, or to stop a behaviour that is having negative consequences and impacts.

Dr. Clarkson provided an example of efficient, direct feedback, addressing Thomas's behavior, specifically:

1. **immediacy** — as soon as he hears about Thomas's behaviour, he addresses the issue

2. **specificity** — Dr. Clarkson is specific as to exactly what behaviour of Thomas' must be stopped

3. **clarity** — Dr. Clarkson does not muddy the waters by incorporating positive feedback with the negative feedback using the *feedback sandwich*.

Many managers have been trained with the *feedback sandwich* where a leader provides positive feedback, followed with negative feedback, and ending with another dash of positive feedback to finish the conversation. This feedback strategy often fails due to the factor of *recency* where the employee most strongly remembers the last thing said to them and the *averaging* factor where an employee tells themselves that overall they are doing a good job.

The strategy of "good news — bad news — good news" of the feedback sandwich does not work effectively with any of the generational groups. It is particularly risky with Generation Y employees who are not used to receiving negative feedback or being held solely responsible for the consequences of their behaviour—they may minimize the negative feedback and focus on the positive feedback at the beginning and end of the conversation.[18]

To ensure the best results when giving feedback as a leader, use the following strategy:

Step One: Describe the negative behaviour you have observed, its immediate negative consequences and short and long-term negative impacts. The more levels of negative impact you can bring to the employee's attention, the quicker the employee will see what they are doing is negatively affecting others or the organization. The negative impact has to be emphasized, particularly with younger employees who have less experience in the workplace and when the consequences of their negative behaviour is less obvious to them.

Step Two: Describe the positive behaviour you wish to see the employee exhibiting, followed by the immediate positive consequences and the short-term and long-term positive impacts to the organization and team.

The most important thing is to have the conversation. Having a clear process to giving negative feedback can make this difficult job easier.

"*I don't understand.
Has someone forgotten
to pay your wages?*"

Mr. Carson

Chapter Ten
Maintaining Accountability

hen the family of Downton Abbey was away, it was protocol to thoroughly clean all the rooms, polish silver and complete other annual tasks that were difficult to do when the family was in residence. On one such occasion, the footmen, Alfred and James, asked Mr. Carson if they would be receiving any time off while the family was away. Mr. Carson reminded them that they were still being paid a full day's wage and the expectation was a full day's work.

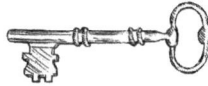

Employees are responsible to perform their duties, not because their manager begs them to, but because they agreed to do so when they accepted the position. A good leader defines the position and its responsibilities at the time of hiring and ensures throughout employment that employees understand and fulfill those expectations. However, without a self-governing work ethic, employees become more difficult to manage if they cannot work independently.

The latest entry into the workforce, Generation Y, has been raised to negotiate everything from bed times to university assignment deadlines.[20] This socialization has predisposed this generation to also anticipate and expect fluidity such as negotiating a break after a busy time.

Although James and Alfred certainly are not members of Generation Y, they exemplify the leadership challenge of employees wanting to negotiate beyond predetermined benefits and rewards. However, rest and rewards outside of labour legislation, collective agreements, and employment contracts, are ultimately at the discretion of the leader.

It is entirely appropriate for a leader to remind an employee of the agreed upon terms of employment—regarding both commitments and compensation.

*"There are rules to this way of life,
Edna. And if you're not prepared
to live by them,
then it's not the right life
for you."*

Mrs. Hughes

Chapter Eleven
Taking Action

dna was hired as a new housemaid while the majority of the family was in Scotland. Mr. Branson and his young daughter were the only family members at home. Edna heard of his past as a chauffeur, noted his good looks, and quickly identified him as her path to upward mobility. She broke several rules of protocol including engaging in personal conversation at an intimate level with Mr. Branson. When she overheard his plans to have lunch at the village pub, she abandoned her duties without permission and conveniently placed herself in his path. Although both of these actions were grounds for discipline, the more egregious offence came when Edna was directed to do a task by her manager and she refused. It was clear at this moment to both Mr. Carson and Mrs. Hughes that Edna was unwilling to follow the rules within the terms of her employment and she was dismissed.

The corporate culture of Downton Abbey was one of clear lines of protocol around relationships above and below stairs, everything ranging from the larger issue of personal relationships down to details as small as the manner of address. The example above was chosen not to discuss personal relationships in the workplace, but to illustrate a leader's responsibility to act when an employee commits a dismissible offence.

Many managers do not like to follow through with discipline or termination for several reasons. In addition to the common **human desire to avoid conflict**, three other reasons may lie within the leader themselves:

1. codependency or secondary gain

2. lack of knowledge

3. lack of preparedness.

Technically, **codependency** is when a person subjugates their needs to the needs of another. Often codependency involves *secondary gain*—where the willingness to do the job as a leader is secondary to what the leader may gain by not doing their job. For example, in a workplace where a manager may be friends or related to an employee, there may be added pressure to allow that employee to remain in the workplace even if the employee has acted in a way which demands discipline or dismissal.

With the advent of Human Resource departments, many managers have abdicated their responsibility to take action in the area of discipline. A leader's **lack of knowledge** of legal obligations, terms, definitions, and policies that govern their employee contracts makes them unable to act as required. As a result, the opportunity for early intervention to reduce the effect of the problem on the individual and team is lost. The leader avoids action, leaving others to clean up the mess. This undermines the leader's credibility and lessens her authority.

Unfortunately, the third reason for inaction, a **lack of preparedness**, may be the most prevalent of those within the leader's control. Due to the daily crisis management that many leaders are faced with, proper documentation and record keeping can fall by the wayside. For progressive discipline, proper documentation must be maintained if the organization is to follow current labour law when terminating an employee. There can be additional paperwork required to meet the terms of a collective agreement in a union environment. Good leaders know they have to do this, but they often don't get it done. As a result of incomplete documentation, a manager is less likely to address a disciplinary issue.

The longer the employee has been with the organization, the harder it may be for the manager to dismiss them—for both legal and emotional reasons. Therefore, the leader should take every opportunity in the 90-day probationary period to properly assess whether or not an employee has the willingness and skills needed to do the job and will be a good fit for the position. This is the leader's chance to craft her team and is the key reason to personally mentor and train a new employee. The probation period, defined by labour law, is a vehicle for the leader to make this decision without the rigorous demands of progressive discipline and the financial cost of severance.

The last and most significant issue that stops leaders from taking action is the **external force of the culture of the organization** itself—whether a lack of resources or the homeostasis of an organization's current dysfunction. If an organization does not have proper staffing levels to accommodate suspended or terminated employees, there will be pressure to keep incompetent or unproductive employees on staff to meet short term customer demands.

Homeostasis is the tendency of an organization to maintain its existing structure and internal systems, even when faced with external changes. A common reason for homeostatic dysfunction is nepotism—where personal relationships entangle the disciplinary process.

If poor leadership performance is ignored due to a human desire to avoid conflict, a lack of preparedness, a lack of knowledge, or a history of inaction—the resulting corporate culture will become toxic and its perpetuating dysfunction inevitable.

If a leader's barrier to taking action is one of the first four internal barriers, she has the power to change. If the leader's barrier is the above external one, she should consider moving to a different organization where she is allowed to hire, develop and maintain a functional work team. If the leader is forced to retain employees who are not doing the job, the effect will spread to fellow employees who will either lower their standards of performance or leave the organization. With a low performing team, the leader will inevitably fail.

Leaders must take action to fix what can be fixed, accept the reality of what cannot be fixed—and if necessary, make a decision to leave.

Leading Culture

Protecting Brand
Respecting Leadership
Perceiving Influence
Professional Relationships
Marshalling Team

"To progress in your chosen career,
William, you must remember
that a good servant at all times
retains a sense of pride and dignity,
that reflects the pride and dignity
of the family he serves."

Mr. Carson

Chapter Twelve
Protecting Brand

fter the death of the heir to the earldom by the sinking of the Titanic, the new heir, Matthew Crawley, had been identified. The family and servants were anxious and excited to meet this young man who would be so influential in all their lives. At the dinner welcoming Matthew Crawley, the staff was on high alert to deliver the best representation of the Grantham brand. The footman, William, was serving at the table and had a small tear on the shoulder seam of his uniform. He had felt the seam go earlier in the evening, but had decided to mend the tear at the end of the night. Mr. Carson, observing the tear, instructed William to mend it immediately and admonished the footman to never appear in public again in such a state of undress.

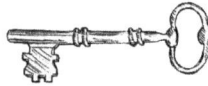

As much as we in business want to define our brand and think we are in control of our brand, our brand is determined by our customer and the public in general. We could list many corporate examples of both strong brands and brands that have been tarnished. Once a brand has been sullied, it is difficult to raise it up to its previous prominence and definition. It is essential, therefore, for a strong brand to make every effort to preserve itself.

The brand of the Earl of Grantham and family was one of prestige, power, and philanthropy. As members of the aristocracy, the family had economic and social power which they were required to use for the benefit and betterment of the people who lived and worked within their estate and county. The Grantham brand was strong, but there was no guarantee it would remain so. Estates fell, both economically and ethically, through mismanagement and negligence by its executive management (aristocratic families). As a senior level of the aristocracy, there was an increased burden and expectation to courageously lead and generously provide. This was demonstrated by the opening of the house as a convalescent home during wartime, establishment and ongoing funding of the local hospital and school, and the development and maintenance of social housing.

This aristocratic protocol of the time of *Downton Abbey* required houses such as the Earl of Grantham's to be maintained at a level to which the King of England could drop by on a moment's notice. The prestige of the brand was maintained by the quality and presentation of food, the calibre of entertainment, the comfort and beauty of the house and grounds, and the dignity and skill of the staff within and without. It is in this context, that William's ripped uniform and Carson's impassioned criticism should be viewed.

What is the role of the leader to maintain the corporate brand? First, to understand it. Secondly, to protect it. In order to protect it, he must clearly see what is the greatest risk. Mr. Carson saw the dress requirements of the staff to be a key vulnerability point to the Grantham brand.

Each industry and organization has within it key points of vulnerability which, if compromised, could be catastrophic to their brand. Consider the case of the Canadian meat producer, Maple Leaf Foods, which enjoyed a strong respected brand until it was brought to its knees with a food safety failure resulting in listeria and a nationwide product recall. In August 2008, Maple Leaf Foods was responsible for one of the worst food-borne disease outbreaks in Canadian history, leaving 21 people dead and more suffering from listeriosis after eating tainted meat products.

Maple Leaf Foods held 21st place with a score of 66/100 on the Marketing/Leger Corporate Reputation Survey. 73% of Canadians said they had a positive opinion of Maple Leaf Foods and only 7% had a negative opinion. Once it was announced that listeria was found in its products and people were dying, Maple Leaf Foods' reputation score immediately dropped from 66/100 to 8/100. Almost half the people surveyed moved from a positive to a negative opinion of the company.[23]

In any food business, food safety is a key vulnerability point to the brand. In the organizational environment, quality processes are regulated and maintained through audit and procedure. As a result, it is within the leader's control to improve those processes to safeguard brand.

But unlike the process of manufacturing at Maple Leaf Foods, where new and stricter protocols were implemented to address the food safety issue, some points of vulnerability are beyond the leader's control to repair, once breached.

Social media and instant communication bring many benefits and cost savings to marketing, but they can also damage brand as quickly as they build it. Consider the damaged brand of the American company, UBER, and its founder and former CEO, Travis Kalanick, who was recorded on video berating a contract driver while sitting in the back seat of a car share vehicle. The corresponding social media storm triggered a series of events that drove the CEO from his role as leader of the organization he created.[24]

Today's leaders must be aware of the key vulnerability points of their brand—whether it is quality control, customer safety issues, labour relations, environment impact or employee banter on Facebook—and be vigilant when and where they can be to protect brand.

"You will therefore please
accord him the respect
he is entitled to."

Lady Grantham

Chapter Thirteen
Respecting Leadership

r. Matthew Crawley (Lord Grantham's third cousin and heir) had recently arrived in Downton. The heir was the future leader of the estate and all the businesses within the enterprise. Miss O'Brien, lady's maid to Lady Grantham, did not feel that Matthew Crawley's credentials warranted his ascending to the position. She decided she would withdraw any support or respect for him as a leader and communicated her disdain for her future employer to her coworkers in the servant's hall (employee staff room). Her comments were overheard by her employer, Lady Grantham, who insisted that Miss O'Brien refer to Matthew Crawley in a manner reflecting his executive leadership role.

In today's workplace, there will always be people who are promoted or hired that other employees believe are not worthy or qualified. Many work environments and cultures become negative and even toxic due to employees who disparage fellow coworkers, leaders, and the organization itself.

It is vital for a leader to clarify to all employees where and when employees are free to speak candidly about the company, its leadership or fellow coworkers. This includes work spaces, coffee rooms, public spaces both inside and outside of the company, and on social media. Without this clarity through direct supervision and feedback, it makes it difficult to discipline or coach employees if negative comments have developed into a toxic culture that supersedes the brand.

A sign of equality in the western workplace is a lack of formality of address. Outside of the political sphere, formality has slowly declined to a casual relationship between superiors and subordinates. Rarely would a manager, except perhaps when involved in a job interview, be addressed as Mr. or Ms. This perspective assumes that the ideal *power distance* between a superior and a subordinate is minimal.

Cross cultural researcher, Geerte Hofstde, coined the phrase *Power Distance* and defined it as "the extent to which the less powerful members of an organization accept and expect that power is distributed unequally". Countries that have high power distance accept the hierarchical order in which people are in the organization and there is no further justification needed to explain who has power.[26]

Robert J. House of the University of Pennsylvania did a substantial research project of 17,300 middle managers in 951 organizations and 62 countries to develop a series of cultural values. The GLOBE study identifies the power distance variable between Canada and three of its primary source countries of immigrants: China, Philippines, and India.[27]

At a score of 94, the Philippines is definitely a hierarchical society, followed by China at 80, and India at 77. With a low score of 39, Canadian workplace culture is marked by a high value placed on equality which is reflected by the lack of overt status or class distinctions.[28]

As our workplaces become more culturally diverse with employees from around the globe, this leadership lesson becomes even more evident. In Asian countries, it is seen as an extremely negative behaviour to disparage your organization or leaders in the workplace or public sphere. This value of hierarchy and formality, along with the expectation that negative feedback is only given privately, may create professional discomfort on behalf of employees who regard disrespecting leadership disconcerting to witness and unthinkable to partake in.

An effective work culture is one where all employees, at every level, treat each other with respect and communicate encouraging conversation.

*"Everyone knows
you can twist him around
your little finger."*

Mrs. Patmore

Chapter Fourteen
Perceiving Influence

rs. Hughes and Mr. Carson were developing a romantic relationship in the workplace. Although they were both at the same level of authority and their feelings were not apparent to all staff members, their colleague, Mrs. Patmore, was aware of their close connection. Mr. Carson was in charge of building the WWI memorial for the village of Downton. Mrs. Patmore's nephew's name was to be omitted from the war memorial in his home town of Farsley because, unlike other soldiers who were killed by the enemy during the war, he was shot for cowardice. To avoid embarrassment for her family and to bring recognition to her fallen nephew, Mrs. Patmore enlisted the aid of Mrs. Hughes to influence Mr. Carson into breaking the rules of the war department to include her nephew's name on the Downton edifice. She believed that Mrs. Hughes could change Mr. Carson's mind due to their romantic relationship. Mrs. Patmore's effort failed, causing unease for everyone involved.

In the *Downton Abbey* example above, we have a colleague asking for a special favour because they perceive that a special relationship creates the opportunity to work around the established policy. Mrs. Patmore assumed that Mrs. Hughes had a high level of influence over Mr. Carson because he and Mrs. Hughes had begun a close personal relationship.

For many decades, organizational policies have discouraged or forbidden romantic relationships between employees in the workplace. The supervisor/subordinate relationship is clearly inappropriate, leaving the leader vulnerable to career-killing sexual harassment suits and costly litigation.

Romantic relationships between colleagues, however, can also be problematic and ultimately counterproductive due to:

1. **Inappropriate personal contact in the workplace:** In our current work world with its heightened sensitivity to sexual harassment, employees are more than ever in tune with how they interact in close physical proximity. Intimate physical touch found usually only in social or private settings, when displayed in the workplace between employees, creates an environment of discomfort for many.

2. **Inappropriate conversations in the workplace:** When strong negative or positive emotions, based on a personal relationship, overflow into the business environment, surrounding employees feel awkward at finding themselves in what seems to be a private moment—instead of a conversation related to work and the legitimate activity designated for that space.

Coworkers may discern a personal relationship between two employees much earlier than it is publicly acknowledged. It is in this period of time that the less subtle, but no less disruptive, perceptions of influence and favouritism bubble to the surface, as did in the case with Mrs. Patmore. Although she had never been told that a romantic relationship existed, she discerned her coworkers' feelings, perceived influence, and attempted to take advantage.

When the perception of influence and visible favouritism becomes apparent and accepted on a widespread basis in an organization, a cultural shift occurs where employees seek promotion and career advancement through the parlaying of personal relationships rather than by good performance and increased productivity.

When career path advancement becomes based on personal relationships, the corporate culture literally becomes "not what you know, but who you know".

With the best of intentions for professionalism, true love can be found in unexpected places. If a leader chooses to engage in a personal relationship with a peer, one of the two involved should seek a different position in an organization that is wholly separate. If the leader merely moves to a different department or an associated company, the perception of influence and favouritism does not disappear, but follows.

"Well I can't see that lasting long."

Miss O'Brien

Chapter Fifteen
Professional Relationships

n the first episode of the television series, viewers meet key characters, including Mr. Bates, the new valet to the Earl of Grantham. Mr. Bates had a long history with the Earl. They served together in the South African war where Mr. Bates suffered an injury, resulting in dependence on a cane for support. When Mr. Bates arrives at Downton to take up his new post, he is met with surprise by Mr. Carson, Miss O'Brien, Thomas, Anna, and Mrs. Patmore. The conversation was as follows:

Mrs. Patmore: *"But what about all them stairs?"*
Mr. Bates: *"I keep telling you, I can manage."*
Anna: *"Of course you can."*
The group disperses except for Carson and O'Brien.

Miss O'Brien: *"Well, I can't see that lasting long."*
Mr. Carson (in a disapproving tone): *"Thank you, Miss O'Brien."*

Thomas was surprised and disappointed in the arrival of Mr. Bates as this meant he would no longer be the acting valet to the Earl of Grantham, with little hope of being assigned the post permanently. He was a co-conspirator to Miss O'Brien and together they attempted to manipulate the downstairs politics. To this end, she wished to remove Mr. Bates from his post to clear the path for Thomas's promotion. Her sarcasm in the quote above was only the beginning of her attempts to use Bates' disability to demean and discredit him.

Although Miss O'Brien's behaviour may have seemed cruel and outdated, sarcasm and innuendo are often used as weapons in the workplace of today. Subtle zingers to malign a colleague's performance or ideas. Faint comments ridiculing another's personal appearance or manner of speaking. Malicious gossip regarding another's reputation, work relationships, and career advancement. Many of these sabotaging tactics are familiar.

As situations arise, humans typically respond out of their stereotypes and worldviews with unconscious communication and behaviour. Sometimes this communication and behaviour is professional and appropriate for the workplace—other times, it is not. Leaders need to be vigilant to build and preserve a positive corporate culture by defining workplace communication and behaviour that is acceptable — and to draw the line when it needs to be drawn, as did Mr. Carson with Miss O'Brien.

In the *Downton Abbey* example above, the characters each respond differently to the disability of Mr. Bates:[31]

1. **Naïveté (Mrs. Patmore)**: Sometimes people move obliviously in the workplace, acting with no knowledge or awareness of the impact of their communication. Mrs. Patmore's comment regarding all the stairs was not meant to demean Mr. Bates, but her genuine concern was based on the assumption that he would be unable to do the job and her question ultimately sounded rude.

2. **Perpetuator (Miss O'Brien)**: Others are fully aware of their inappropriate comments or behaviours, but are deliberate in their disparagement or simply do not care about the impact on others. Miss O'Brien perceives that comments she makes about Mr. Bates will not impact her, as she believes her role as ladies' maid to Lady Grantham is unassailable.

3. **Silent Supporter (Thomas)**: Some tolerate the unjust behaviour towards others if they secretly agree with it; others avoid the conversation in an attempt to not become involved. Thomas does not comment at the time, silently supporting Miss O'Brien's attempt to humiliate Mr. Bates as he knows he himself cannot lead the campaign to have Mr. Bates removed from the position as valet.

4. **Risk Taker (Anna)**: Some take action when they think others are speaking or acting inappropriately, even though it may affect their own job security. Anna plays this role, defending Mr. Bates and his ability to do the job.

In the example above, Mr. Carson shuts down the comment by O'Brien, reminding her that he expects conversation to remain professional in the servants' hall. By leaders understanding how people respond they can take action to encourage, discourage, and discipline where appropriate. For example:

1. **Naiveté:** Employees may not realize that their behaviour is based on stereotypes and may be offensive. They may unknowingly breach policy regarding discrimination or harassment. A leader is responsible to help their employees to understand what can and cannot be communicated in the workplace, regardless if the communication is conscious or unconscious.

2. **Perpetuator:** Some employees are aware of their stereotypes and prejudices and that their behaviour may be offensive. They believe that there will be no negative consequences to what they say or do. They continue with derogatory comments and actions as if policy does not apply to them. The leader's role is to call them out, clearly communicate what is acceptable and use discipline if the perpetuator fails to follow policy.

3. **Avoider:** Employees in this category are aware of the stereotypes their coworkers hold. They may or may not have negative stereotypes of their own. They are reluctant to address the inappropriate behaviour of others because they either agree with the behaviour or want to stay out of the situation altogether. Either way, their silence is perceived as supporting the inappropriate behaviour. A leader needs to bring these employees into the fold and be sure that policy and behavioural norms are communicated and call upon employees for positive contribution when their silence is deafening.

4. **Risk Takers:** These employees are aware of stereotypes held both by themselves and others. They are also aware of the negative impact on the work team and culture. They are willing to take action to encourage an environment of respect and harmony for themselves and others. Leaders should support and encourage employees who are taking risks to create a better workplace.

Leaders know the workplace is an constantly changing complex environment which they are charged with shepherding into civil discourse and increased productivity. To ensure professional relationships, a leader must champion respectful dialogue and behaviour.

"We'll all pull together and it'll be great fun."

Lady Grantham

Chapter Sixteen
Marshalling Team

A grand dinner was planned at Downton Abbey to entertain prominent guests and remind Mrs. Levinson (Lady Grantham's mother from America) of the importance and purpose of the earldom and estate— with the goal that she would invest further in its maintenance, stability and growth. The table was set, the guests had arrived—and the oven was broken. Mrs. Hughes and Mr. Carson called Lady Grantham to the side to inform her that none of the food was cooked, nor would it be. Soon Lady and Lord Grantham and Mrs. Levinson put their heads together to devise a solution to save the evening's event and fulfill the guests' expectations—a moving indoor picnic with group singing as entertainment. In order to succeed, all staff were required to be engaged in kitchen duties, for which many were untrained. The servants' duties at Downton Abbey were very defined and it was rare for someone to function out of their designated role and move into someone else's tasks. As a result, Mr. Carson, Mrs. Hughes, Mrs. Patmore, Lady Grantham—and even Mrs. Levinson—marshalled the staff to tackle the mission at hand. Supported and encouraged to function in this different way, the team was able to produce an evening that, even for Mr. Carson with his exacting standards, was considered a success.

Day-to-day productivity in an organization demands defined roles and clear boundaries—but in a time of crisis, tasks and duties can be shared or reallocated. In today's workplace, crisis can happen at any time. Not only do staff need to be prepared to use their talents in different ways and places, but they also have to be willing to do so.

This is why it is essential for a leader during any employment contract or collective agreement negotiation to clearly define what is meant by "additional duties as assigned" because the last thing any leader needs to hear in a moment of crisis is, "That's not my job!"

The role of the leader is to ensure that employees understand the big picture, the pieces and how they fit together, how each position affects other positions, how a crisis anywhere belongs to everyone, and how a loss incurred anywhere is owned by everyone.

Marshalling the team to work together in a crisis requires a two-part strategy:

Questions to pose when marshalling a team during a crisis:

1. Who is best able to fix this crisis?

2. Is there anyone else specifically qualified to assist the people identified in question #1 who can participate directly in that work?

3. What regular tasks, assigned to those identified in question #1 and question #2, are non-essential to solving the problem and can be carved off and reassigned to others?

4. Who in the organization can complete some or all of the regular tasks identified in question #3?

5. What supports can be provided to those identified in question #1 and #2 to more easily and efficiently fix the crisis and who can provide these supports?

Questions to ask once the crisis has been resolved:

1. Did the people who solved the crisis directly or the people who supported them incur any overtime that needs to be paid out or offered in lieu?

2. How will the uninvolved staff be made aware of the extra effort expended by those who solved the crisis and preserved corporate brand?

3. How will the leader communicate information about the crisis for the purpose of educating employees, prepare for a similar

crisis, show gratitude for those who went the extra mile, and build on the cultural values of teamwork and responsibility?

Unfortunately many organizations have a cultural dynamic where a small number of employees carry the heavy load of picking up the pieces when crisis strikes, no matter where the source or what the cause.

This negative organizational dynamic fosters resentment between departments. A corporate culture will either encourage or discourage the development of silos—where individuals and their departments work in smug isolation from one another.

An effective corporate culture is comprised of employees who respect boundaries and roles and can still move from independence to interdependence in order to address crisis.

Leading With Others

Respecting Boundaries
Common Purpose
Allowing Support
Intentional Partnering

"I'm not sure
that you're entitled
to dress down Mrs. Patmore
in this way."

Mrs. Hughes

Chapter Seventeen
Respecting Boundaries

rs. Crawley hired Downton Abbey's former housemaid Ethel as a cook. Since leaving Downton Abbey, single mother Ethel had fallen on hard times and resorted to prostitution to provide for her young son. In an attempt to assist Ethel to rebuild her life, Mrs. Crawley inadvertently caused herself and Crawley House to become subjects of gossip for the surrounding village. In an effort to protect the reputation of Downton Abbey, Mr. Carson instructed all the staff to steer clear of Crawley House and not to associate with Ethel.

Mrs. Crawley had planned a luncheon for the ladies of the family. In an effort to please her employer and guests, Ethel enlisted the aid of Mrs. Patmore in planning the menu and instruction in preparing it. While on errands in the village, Mr. Carson spied Mrs. Patmore leaving Crawley House. With Mrs. Hughes later in the day, he confronted Mrs. Patmore who admitted that she has been helping Ethel. When Mr. Carson vehemently objected to Mrs. Patmore's activity and suggested she was frolicking with a prostitute, Mrs. Patmore was offended at the suggestion. Mrs. Hughes intervened, saying, "Mr. Carson, I'm not sure that you're entitled to dress down Mrs. Patmore in this way."

As the head of staff, it was within Mr. Carson's right to question Mrs. Patmore's presence at Crawley House, but it was not within his authority to forbid her from helping Ethel or being at Crawley House. To add insult to injury, he made a vulgar suggestion that by her assisting Ethel, she herself had diminished her own character.

Mrs. Hughes and Mrs. Patmore both reported directly to Lady Grantham and were not Mr. Carson's subordinates, but rather his peers. If Mrs. Patmore was to be disciplined for inappropriate behavior, it would be from executive management, not Mr. Carson.

Lines of authority, as clearly evident in the *Downton Abbey* example above, have been blurred by today's flattened organizations, collaborative work teams, and the shift away from formal authority. It was easy for Mrs. Hughes to legitimately remind Mr. Carson of the boundaries of their individual roles as senior managers. In today's workplaces, sometimes those boundaries are not so obvious.

The outcome of interference in a peer's **tasks and duties, decisions** and **relationships** can be damaging to both peer relationships and productivity if individuals take action to keep others at a distance to avoid interference and judgment:

Tasks and Duties: Organizational charts exist for a reason. Tasks and duties are divided in an organization among departments to maximize efficiency and productivity for the benefit of the organization and their customers. A leader must focus on his own area of responsibility, and not the areas of others. To engage in the tasks and duties of another department because a leader finds it more interesting or believes he has a better or quicker way to get the job done results in duplication of work and risks the health of the peer relationship in question. If a leader finds an area more appealing than his current role, he needs to make an effort to pursue leadership in that department through future job opportunities when available, rather than highjacking another leader's domain.

Decisions: In the case above with Mrs. Patmore and Mr. Carson, there was a protocol as to how the leaders questioned their peers' decisions. Leaders are generally unaware of the motivation and mitigating factors behind the decisions of their peers. If a leader requires more information, the conversation should be in person, in private, and in a respectful tone.

Relationships: Peers are a leader's first point of contact within other departments or business areas. If there is an issue that needs to be addressed, a leader should notify his peer before investigating directly with that leader's staff. If someone reaches out to a leader's superior or subordinate without them being aware of the issue at hand, it may undermine the leader's authority and ability to solve future problems. Peers need to support each other by respecting boundaries and position whenever possible.

In today's competitive business environment, successful organizations do not have time to waste on dysfunctional leadership teams. Leaders must value their peer relationships because in moments of crisis, these coworkers may be the only people who can help achieve a successful outcome.

Only by understanding our peers' roles and relationships can we know and respect their boundaries.

"I just want what's best for the village."

Dr. Clarkson

"At least we have that in common."

Lady Grantham

Chapter Eighteen
Common Purpose

D r. Clarkson and Lady Grantham were both decision makers on the board of the local village hospital. The larger Royal Yorkshire Hospital had proposed a merger, but Lady Grantham and Dr. Clarkson had different views of which direction to take. Lady Grantham wanted to explore the possibility of merging with the Royal Yorkshire Hospital. She saw it as an opportunity to gain better healthcare for the village with access to the new methods, treatments, machines and advances that had been made since the war that were beyond the village hospital budget. Dr. Clarkson, however, believed the best healthcare for the village was one that was locally managed and delivered. He had concerns about a possible loss of services resulting from being tied to a larger establishment. He even told Mrs. Crawley that, *"Once they take over the hospital, they will lay down the law with no regard for the needs of this area. I have seen it in war and peace. It is always the same."*[35]

In the above conflict, Lady Grantham and Dr. Clarkson slowly found common ground. They were unconsciously using a Neuro Linguistic Programming (NLP) strategy called *chunking up.*

When two people are stuck in an argument or negotiation where they are challenged to find common areas of agreement, this strategy can come to the rescue.[36] *Chunking up* refers to moving to more general or abstract pieces of information. *Chunking down* means moving to more specific or detailed information. To chunk up on a piece of information, a leader can ask the following questions: What is the intention? For what purpose? Why is this important?

In the example above, the levels of chunking that may have been in Lady Grantham's mind were:

- Merge with the larger hospital—why is this important?
- So we can have up-to-date modern equipment—why is this important?
- So we can provide quality care—why is this important?
- To create a village of healthy citizens.

In Dr. Clarkson's mind, the levels of chunking may have been:

- Keep the decision making local—why is this important?
- So we can designate expenditures to local needs—why is this important?
- So we can provide quality care—why is this important?
- To create a village of healthy citizens.

In the end, both Lady Grantham and Dr. Clarkson wanted what was best for the village's citizens.

Chunking up is a very useful tool when engaging in both negotiation and mediation. Far too often in negotiations, individuals continue to explore solutions at a level of detail at which they disagree. By *chunking up* until both parties agree, individuals can then build on the common purpose and move down into details while in rapport, knowing they have a shared goal.

In today's world, dialogue often seems more heated and polarized than ever before. Thanks to snipes on social media and sound bites in the 24-hour news cycle, individuals are tempted to not only entrench themselves in one side of the argument, but to attribute negative—even sinister, motives to the other side.

Leaders have the responsibility to seek a common purpose, even when it is illusive to find. To a leader's surprise, she may find there is a common goal and the conflict is in the "how", not the "why".

The real key to achieving results with peers is to remember—we are all on the same side.

*"I could almost manage ...
I don't need a doctor to tell me
I'm going blind."*

Mrs. Patmore

Chapter Nineteen
Allowing Support

rs. Patmore had been slowly losing her sight due to cataracts. She believed she was going blind and when it finally happened it will be the end of her career—who had ever heard of a blind cook? She denied that she was losing her ability to see and was beginning to make significant errors. She blamed others for her mistakes, specifically the kitchen maid, Daisy. As each disaster occurred, the surrounding staff covered up the incident. Finally, during a dinner party where Mrs. Patmore generously covered the pudding with salt instead of sugar, she was exposed.

Mrs. Patmore: *"I know that pudding! I chose it 'cos I know it!"*
Mrs. Hughes: *"Which is why you wouldn't let her ladyship have the pudding she wanted. Because you didn't know it."*[38]

Mrs. Patmore: *"I could almost manage for a long time. Knowing the kitchen and where everything was kept. Even with that fool girl."*
Mr. Carson: *"I think you might owe Daisy an apology."*[39]

Mr. Carson: *"And you've not been to a doctor?"*
Mrs. Patmore: *"I don't need a doctor to tell me I'm going blind. A blind cook, Mr. Carson. What a joke. Whoever heard of such a thing?"*[40]

Three behaviours, displayed by Mrs. Patmore, illustrate how she as a leader not only jeopardized the success of her department, but also jeopardized her own career security:

1. She **entrenched** herself in the areas that she knew so she was not exposed. She only cooked the recipes she knew by heart, as she could not see to read or prepare new recipes. This limited her ability to be an effective executive chef and manage her team.

2. She **blamed her employees** for her mistakes, alienating them and causing conflict in the team.

3. She was **unwilling to pursue the true cause** of her ailment and the possible treatments or lack thereof due to the fear that the outcome would be negative.

Mrs. Patmore's failure to accept her limitation demanded that the surrounding staff and her peers needed to work harder and respond to the continuing crisis events that she created daily. Ultimately, due to her unwillingness to act to address her declining capacity, Mrs. Patmore's peers and her employer were forced to make the decision for her. Lord Grantham eventually sent her to London to see an eye specialist, hired another cook to cover her duties, and took the matter out of her hands.

Mrs. Patmore's actions to cover up her condition resulted in her positioning herself as a victim in the minds of her staff, peers, and employer. This victimization compromised her credibility as a leader far more than her blindness would have done.

Mrs. Patmore had multiple opportunities to lean on her peers, but instead choose to keep both Mr. Carson and Mrs. Hughes in the dark. If she had allowed support, her peers could have helped her plan and strategize to ensure the needs of her department were being met, even as she struggled with this personal issue.

Life happens to us. We have health problems. We have family issues. Although we are tempted to function as islands separated by miles of sea, good relationships with our peers can be the bridges connecting us all.

"If we each do
what we can do,
then Downton has a real chance."

Mr. Branson

Chapter Twenty
Intentional Partnering

atthew Crawley and Lord Grantham co-managed the estate and hired Mr. Branson as the agent. All three had strong personalities with different skills and backgrounds. Lord Grantham, who had made several poor financial management decisions, thought the organization should stay in its present form and change slowly, respecting and retaining the current tenant contracts. Matthew, who was a corporate lawyer by training, felt that a radical reorganization was necessary to bring the estate into intensive farming and maximize the production on the land, even at the cost of current tenant relationships. Mr. Branson, who had an understanding of farming and a concern for the tenant farmers, believed the window to move to intensive farming was now as the estate currently had the cash available to compensate the tenant farmers. These different views created conflict amongst the three leaders as each attempted to convince the others of the merit of his position.

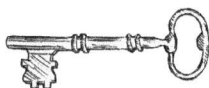

As leaders, we end up partnering with others on projects or problems. Often these partnerships are created in a moment of crisis, leaving the leaders little or no time to discuss how they will work together effectively. Even in the case where two leaders have much in common, there can be disagreement as to the goals, roles, rules of engagement, and how conflict will be resolved—if and when it occurs.

In every partnership situation, the leaders should take time to determine the following:

Goals — why are we coming together to work on this project?

After a heated conversation between Lord Grantham, Matthew Crawley and Mr. Branson regarding the path forward, the goal question was best articulated by Lady Grantham's question, *"But isn't the most important thing, for them (the tenants) or us, is to maintain Downton as a source of employment?"*[42]

Roles — what are the roles necessary and who has the most appropriate skills and talent to each role?

In the *Downton Abbey* example above, Mr. Branson identified that he had experience in farming, Matthew understood business, and Lord Grantham understood the relationships between the executive management and the other stakeholders.

Rules of Engagement — how will we work together and treat each while on the road to achieving these goals?

When there is agreement on goals and roles, there is minimum conflict in partnerships. But when a leader chooses to muddle through without addressing these essential partnering questions, his desire to realize his agenda can cause him to communicate negatively and overstep.

When a person feels that they are not being respected or listened to, they are tempted to communicate in a negative or disrespectful manner. When Lord Grantham failed to convince the others to retain the tenant contracts as they had been in the past, he felt outnumbered, overridden, and disrespected. He then chose to retreat instead of engaging with the other leaders to ensure a successful outcome, *"You seem to be agreed that there's no place for me in all this. So obviously it's time for me to take a back seat."*[43]

Lord Grantham had found himself co-leading after years of being the sole decision maker within the enterprise. Many leaders who have carried the full weight of responsibility find themselves struggling when required to share decision making and turf with others. It is important for a leader to remember the qualities that make him successful when leading independently may be the very qualities that sabotage him when leading in partnership.

Resolution — once there is conflict and leaders have disengaged, how will we resolve the situation?

In the *Downton Abbey* example, Mr. Branson challenged Lord Grantham and reminded him, *"I am a hard worker and I've some knowledge of the land. Matthew knows the law and the nature of business ... You understand the responsibilities we owe to the people round here, those who work for the estate and those that don't. It seems to me that if we could manage to pool all of that, if we each do what we can do, then Downton has a real chance."*[44]

Lord Grantham reconsiders his position and re-engages in the partnership, telling Matthew, *"Let's give it a go, and see what the future brings."*[45]

Great leaders know that they don't know everything. Great leaders hire and partner with people who have the strengths, knowledge and talents they lack.

Conclusion

eadership is neither easy nor clear cut. It can be confusing to know where to find the best advice. As discussed in the Introduction, it can be useful to look into the past to find solutions for problems in the present.

Effective leadership requires insight, self-discipline, courage, and influence.

- **Insight:** the leader's ability to know themselves and those around them

- **Self-discipline:** the leader's ability to discipline their behaviour and communication when necessary

- **Courage:** the leader's ability to act when necessary

- **Influence:** the leader's ability to work with employees, peers, and superiors to get the job done.[46]

There are examples in this book of these characteristics and how essential they are to a leader's career fulfillment. Whether you call yourself a leader, a manager or a boss—a return to the basics of honesty, clear communication, boundaries and respectful behavior will always decrease your problems and increase your results.

The leaders in *Downton Abbey* managed through turbulent times and a dramatic change in their organization. They not only survived but thrived, providing stability and a new direction for the organization, its employees, and the community at large.

What ensured their success was the clarity under which they functioned, the self-discipline which they applied, and the mutual respect which they observed—each and every day.

Notes and References

Introduction

1. "What Leaders Really Do", *Harvard Business Review* (May-June 1990). Written by J. Kotter

Chapter One

2. Opening Quote: "It will be a huge wrench for me to leave Downton." *Downton Abbey — The Complete Scripts — Season Two* (2013). Written by Julian Fellowes, Page 333

3. Values Congruence and Differences Between the Interplay of Personal and Organizational Value Systems, *Journal of Business Ethics* (1993). Written by B. Z. Posner and W.H. Schmidt

Chapter Two

4. Opening Quote: "He threatened to expose my past, to make me a laughing stock in this house, and in my vanity and pride, I gave him what he wanted." *Downton Abbey — The Complete Scripts — Season One* (2012). Written by Julian Fellowes, Page 118

5. How Often Do People Tend to Lie on Resumes, *Statistic Brain Institute*. Last sourced at: https://www.cpsa.com/resources/articles/how-often-do-people-tend-to-lie-on-resumes and http://www.statisticbrain.com/resume-falsification-statistics/

Chapter Three

6. Opening Quote: "I am having (me) career backwards." "Me" was substituted with "my". Although a common method of language at the time of *Downton Abbey*, when read in isolation is often seen as a typo. (Downton Abbey, The Television Series, Season 4, Episode 3)

7. Longer to launch: Demographic changes in life-course transitions, *Ways of Living: Work, Community and Lifestyle Choices* (2010). Written by R. Venne, Pages 75-98

Chapter Four

8. Opening Quote: "Of course I am concerned, Carson, and you must help me. You know how dear you are to me, and if there are changes that need to be made, we mustn't be afraid to face them." (Downton Abbey, The Television Series, Season 6, Episode 9) **Chapter Five**

9. Opening Quote: "I've an idea that when you mentioned Mrs. Harding's connection with us, you were trying to catch her out. I don't like to see such things, Barrow. I don't care for a lack of generosity." (Downton Abbey, The Television Series, Season 6, Episode 4)

10. Samuel Johnson was an English writer who made lasting contributions to English literature as a poet, essayist, moralist, literary critic, biographer, editor and lexicographer. Johnson was described by the *Oxford Dictionary of National Biography* as "arguably the most distinguished man of letters in English history". Johnson's *A Dictionary of the English Language* was published in 1755. It had a far-reaching effect on Modern English and has been described as "one of the greatest single achievements of scholarship". Until the completion of the Oxford English Dictionary, 150 years later, Johnson's was viewed as the pre-eminent British dictionary.

11. Emily Post published her first etiquette book, *Etiquette in Society, in Business, in Politics, and at Home*, in 1922 and it became a bestseller, with updated versions continuing to be popular for decades. Post spoke on radio programs and wrote a column on good taste which appeared daily in some 200 newspapers, starting in the 1930s. Such books had always been popular in America, but Post's etiquette books went far beyond those of her predecessors.

Chapter Six

12. Opening Quote: "No, I won't be coming. If I came, they wouldn't have fun. They'd spend the day looking over their shoulder ... I'm their leader." *Downton Abbey — The Complete Scripts — Season 3* (2014). Written by Julian Fellowes, Page 509

13. "Law Suits and PR Nightmares: Why Employees Need Social Media Guidelines, *SearchEngineJournal.com* (August 19, 2009). Written by Matt Leonard. Last sourced at: https://www.searchenginejournal.com/why-employees-need-social-media-guidelines/12588/

Chapter Seven

14. Opening Quote: "Mr. Carson has been a kind and wonderful teacher." (Downton Abbey, The Television Series, Season 4, Episode 6)

15. *Escape from Oz: Leadership for the 21st Century* (2001). Written by Jeanne Martinson

Chapter Eight

16. Opening Quote: "It's not nothing, is it?" *Downton Abbey — The Complete Scripts — Season 2* (2013). Written by Julian Fellowes, Page 545

Chapter Nine

17. Opening Quote: "I hear you are becoming mighty imperious in your manner with the staff here, Daisy in particular...there's no need for rudeness. So mind what I say." *Downton Abbey — The Complete Scripts — Season 2* (2013). Written by Julian Fellowes, Page 238

18. *Generation Y and the New Work Ethic* (2013). Written by Jeanne Martinson

Chapter Ten

19. Opening Quote: "I don't understand. Has someone forgotten to pay your wages?" *Downton Abbey — The Complete Scripts — Season 3* (2014). Written by Julian Fellowes, Page 482

20. *Generation Y and the New Work Ethic* (2013). Written by Jeanne Martinson

Chapter Eleven

21. Opening quote: "But there are rules to this way of life, Edna. And if you're not prepared to live by them, then it's not the right life for you." *Downton Abbey — The Complete Scripts — Season 3* (2014). Written by Julian Fellowes, Page 549

Chapter Twelve

22. Opening quote: "To progress in your chosen career William, you must remember that a good servant at all times retains

a sense of pride and dignity, that reflects the pride and dignity of the family he serves." *Downton Abbey — The Complete Scripts — Season 1* (2012). Written by Julian Fellowes, Page 90

23. Damage Control, *www.MarketingMaga.ca.* (May 25, 2009). Written by Dave Scholz

24. Storm of activities between February 28th (when a dashcam video catches CEO Travis Kalanick in a heated argument with a UBER driver over prices) and June 20th (when Kalanick resigns): He apologizes regarding the dashcam incident and says he'll seek leadership help, VP of Product and Growth (Ed Baker) quits, head of AI Labs (Gary Marcus) quits, President of Shareriding (Jeff Jones) quits, UBER temporarily suspends its self-driving car program after a crash in Arizona, a visit to a Seoul escort-karaoke bar by Kalanick and other UBER executives is revealed, VP of Maps and Business Platform (Brian McClendon) and SVP of Communications and Policy (Rachel Whetstone) quit, VP of Global Vehicle Programs (Sherif Marakby) quits, Apple warns UBER it would pull the UBER app off the app store if UBER didn't quit violating Apple policies, GM for New York City (Josh Mohrer) and Head of Finance (Gaulam Gupta) quit, Head of Asia Business (Eric Alexander) and SVP of Business (Emil Michael) quit.

Chapter Thirteen

25. Opening Quote: "You will therefore please accord him the respect he is entitled to." *Downton Abbey — The Complete Scripts — Season 1* (2012). Written by Julian Fellowes, Page 101

26. *From Away — Immigration to Effective Workplace Integration* (2017). Written by Jeanne Martinson, Page 106

27. *From Away — Immigration to Effective Workplace Integration* (2017). Written by Jeanne Martinson, Page 106

28. *From Away — Immigration to Effective Workplace Integration* (2017). Written by Jeanne Martinson, Page 106

Chapter Fourteen

29. Opening quote: "Everyone knows you can twist him around your little finger." (Downton Abbey, The Television Series, Season 5, Episode 3)

Chapter Fifteen

30. Opening Quote: "Well I can't see that lasting long." *Downton Abbey — The Complete Scripts — Season 1*, (2012). Written by Julian Fellowes, Page 18

31. Adapted from: *Diversity Awareness Profile*, (2007). John Wiley & Sons

Chapter Sixteen

32. Opening Quote: "We'll all pull together and it'll be great fun." *Downton Abbey — The Complete Scripts — Season 3*, (2014). Written by Julian Fellowes, Page 125

Chapter Seventeen

33. Opening quote: "Mr. Carson, I'm not sure that you're entitled to dress down Mrs. Patmore in this way." *Downton Abbey — The Complete Scripts — Season 3* (2014). Written by Julian Fellowes, Page 340

Chapter Eighteen

34. Opening quote: "I just want what's best for the village." And "At least we have that in common." (Downton Abbey, The Television Series, Season 6, Episode 2)

35. Downton Abbey, The Television Series Season 6, Episode 1

36. *Time Line Therapy and the Basis of Personality* (1988). Tad James and Wyatt Woodsmall

Chapter Nineteen

37. Opening Quote: "I could almost manage .... I don't need a doctor to tell me I'm going blind." *Downton Abbey — The Complete Scripts — Season 1* (2012), Page 279

38. *Downton Abbey — The Complete Scripts — Season 1* (2012), Page 276

39. *Downton Abbey — The Complete Scripts — Season 1* (2012), Page 279

40. *Downton Abbey — The Complete Scripts — Season 1* (2012), Page 279

Chapter Twenty

41. Opening quote: "If we each do what we can do, then Downton has a real chance." *Downton Abbey — The Complete Scripts — Season 3*, (2014). Written by Julian Fellowes, Page 459

42. *Downton Abbey — The Complete Scripts — Season 3* (2014). Written by Julian Fellowes, Page 453

43. *Downton Abbey — The Complete Scripts — Season 3* (2014). Written by Julian Fellowes, Page 453

44. *Downton Abbey — The Complete Scripts — Season 3* (2014). Written by Julian Fellowes, Page 459

45. "All right. Let's give it a go, and see what the future brings." *Downton Abbey — The Complete Scripts — Season 3* (2014). Written by Julian Fellowes, Page 473

Conclusion

46. *Escape from Oz: Leadership for the 21st Century* (2001). Written by Jeanne Martinson

Acknowledgements

We would like to thank our great team of editors who read our first draft. Their invaluable feedback has much improved this book in your hands. Thanks so much to Alda Bouvier, Malcolm Bucholtz, Pamela Burns, Pat Dell, Laurie Hutchison, Carolyn Schur, and Carole Stepenoff.

Thanks to Margo Davidson-Wood for her wonderful technical support.

Last, but not least, we thank Julian Fellowes for his brilliant characters, eloquent dialogue, and masterful storytelling.

Looking for more
Lessons From *Downton Abbey?*
Book Two

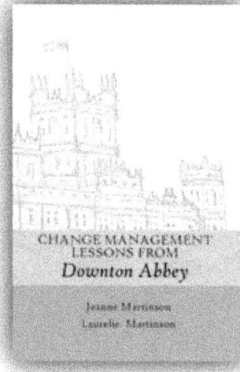

Change Management
Lessons From *Downton Abbey*

Section One: Shifting Technology

Filter the Data — *"I find the whole idea a kind of thief of life."*
Evaluate the Costs — *"A telephone is not a toy, but a useful and valuable tool."*
Recognize the Emotions — *"It makes her part of the future
and leaves me stuck in the past."*
Figure It Out — *"I had it up too high, but I've got the hang of it now."*

Section Two: Shifting Roles

Change the People — *"It must be so hard to meet the challenge of the future,
and yet be fair."*
Find the People — *"So I told them I will do it, I will drive the tractor."*
Move On — *"Service is ending for most of us."*
Make the Change — *"I want to leave service. I want to be a secretary."*
Create Your Opportunity — *"Well, I'll rent it out now and, then later, I
thought I might take in some lodgers."*

Section Three: Shifting Culture

Keep the House in Order — *"The estate has been run very wastefully."*

Mind the Surroundings — *"The wage bill is three times what it was before the war."*

Sell the Change — *"You are a good spokesman for Matthew's vision. Better than he has been."*

Do No Harm — *"She would be willing the changes to fail."*

Making It Stick — *"His lordship will retreat to his old ways and abandon all Mr. Matthew's reforms."*

Facebook: Lessons from Downton Abbey

Email: *LessonsFromDowntonAbbey@sasktel.net*

Publisher: WoodDragonBooks.com

Looking for more
Lessons From *Downton Abbey?*
Book Three

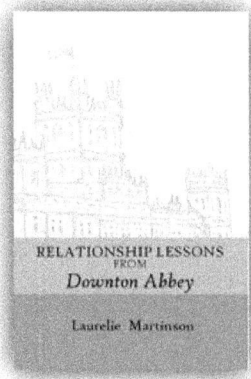

Relationship
Lessons From *Downton Abbey*

Section One: Loving Spouses

Loving Long — *"Marriage is a long business."*
Loving Complements — *"We were a marriage of equals."*
Loving Exclusively — *"You let him into your private life."*
Loving Honestly — *"Would you have married me in a lie?"*

Section Two: Loving Parents

Loving Fairly — *"I love my children equally."*
Loving Courageously — *"There is more than one kind of good mother."*
Loving Spaces — *"I have decided to go away ... and return when I have gained control of my tongue."*
Loving Intercession — *"Somehow we must find Edith and we must hear from her what she wants."*

Section Three: Loving Friends

Faithful Friendship — *"Now that you've accepted him,*
You'll hear no argument from me."
Gracious Friendship — *"You saved me from making a fool of myself."*
Dedicated Friendship — *"We must stick together. Your dream is my dream*
now."
Resilient Friendship — *"I need to be sure we can disagree without there being*
any bad feeling between us."

Section Four: Loving Siblings

Granting Freedom — *"Make the right choice for you and not for us."*
Abiding Loyalty — *"Then be on my side!"*
Reliable Forgiveness — *"I assumed you would be fairly sorry*
unless you're actually insane."
Loving Longest — *"Because in the end, you're my sister."*

Facebook: Lessons from Downton Abbey

Email: *LessonsFromDowntonAbbey@sasktel.net*

Publisher: WoodDragonBooks.com

Jeanne Martinson

eanne Martinson is a professional speaker, trainer and best-selling author who has worked internationally and throughout Canada. Since co-founding her own firm, MARTRAIN Corporate and Personal Development in 1993, Jeanne has inspired thousands of participants in her keynote presentations and workshops with her humour, insight and real-world examples.

Jeanne completed her Master of Arts degree in Leadership at Royal Roads University in Victoria, British Columbia, Canada. (Her graduate research focused on the differences and similarities of criminal gang leaders and corporate leaders). Jeanne also holds a Certificate in Organizational Behaviour from Heriot-Watt University (Edinburgh, Scotland) and is certified as a practitioner of NLP (Neuro Linguistic Programming).

Jeanne delivers workshops and keynote addresses to government, associations and the private sector. Her most popular topics are leadership and diversity. As a Canadian bestselling author and strategist in workplace diversity, Jeanne's goal is to assist leaders in understanding diversity issues so they may attract, retain and engage their ideal workforce.

Jeanne takes a leading role in her community, a dedication that was recognized with the Canada 125 Medal, the YWCA Women of Distinction Award, the Centennial Leadership Award (for outstanding contribution to the Province of Saskatchewan), the Athena Award, and the EMCY (the national Diversity award of Canada).

Jeanne has eleven books in print, including:

From Away — Immigration to Effective Workplace Integration which explores the differences between Eastern and Western business mindsets and how those differences affect hiring, leading, and retaining new employees who are immigrants from Asia.

Generation Y and the New Ethic gives concrete information about the different generations found in the workplace today with a focus on work ethic and the motivations and values of Generation Y.

Escape from Oz — Leadership For The 21st Century explores the parallels of the characters in the fable *The Wonderful Wizard of Oz* and our own beliefs about personal and professional leadership.

War & Peace in the Workplace — Diversity, Conflict, Understanding, Reconciliation explores how workplaces are becoming more diverse, how diversity may trigger conflict, and how we can prevent diversity-based conflict from spiraling down into dysfunction.

Tossing the Tiara: Keys to Creating Powerful Women Leaders includes an update on the research from Jeanne's first book, *Lies and Fairy Tales That Deny Women Happiness*, and adds information on gender gap, the impact of news media, and the continuing influence of the Disney princess phenomenon.

Managing #MeToo — Balancing Employee Protection and Corporate Brand explores the good, the bad, and the ugly of the #MeToo movement and provides strategies for leaders and individuals to manage sexual harassment issues in the workplace.

Hemingway or Twain? Unleashing Your Author Personality is a book to help non-fiction book authors get their book completed with less stress, time and money.

Contact Jeanne at

Email: watertiger@sasktel.net

Telephone: 1.306.59.7993

www.martrain.org

Laurelie Martinson

aurelie Martinson is a communication and behaviour specialist with 25 years of experience working with business, government and community organizations. During her years working as a consultant and teaching management communications at the University of Regina, she continued to coach leaders and employees in the discipline of maintaining personal well-being in the wake of organizational change. Her provocative programs carved a pathway for leaders and employees to improve communication in both hostile and well-functioning environments.

Laurelie developed a model of *Generational Addiction and Dependency* that was used as core training for Saskatchewan Social Services. After years of leading group therapy sessions on issues surrounding codependency, recovery, and spiritual development, Laurelie continues to challenge her clients to accept the consequences of their choices, communication and behaviour—and take the necessary steps to rebuild relationships on the foundations of truth, accountability, and compassion.

Laurelie studied at the University of Saskatchewan and is continuing graduate studies in Ministry Leadership and Counseling at Alberta Bible College.

Contact Laurelie at

Email: schoolingfish@sasktel.net
Facebook: Schooling Fish & **YouTube:** Wise Words

Lessons from *Downton Abbey*
Book Series

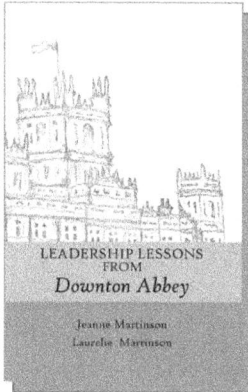

Downton Abbey is an iconic British television series that captivated the world with its portrayal of the transition of family, society and organizational life during the years immediately before and after WWI.

Not only did it sweep away its viewers with dramatic characters, eye catching costumes and cinematography, it provided lessons that can be applied to our world today.

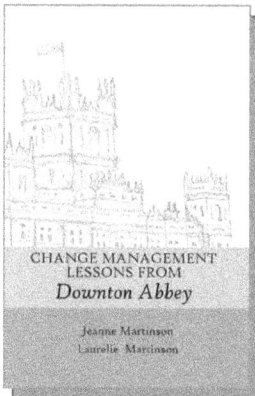

This book series uses illustrations from Downton Abbey to communicate timeless wisdom that can improve our personal and professional lives.

Leadership Lessons from
Downton Abbey

Change Management Lessons from
Downton Abbey

Relationship Lessons from
Downton Abbey

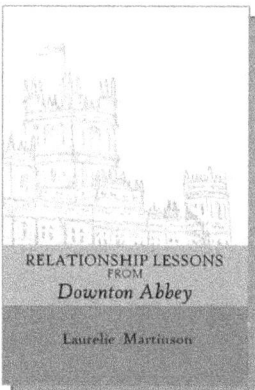

Facebook:
Lessons from Downton Abbey

Email:
LessonsFromDowntonAbbey@sasktel.net

Publisher:
WoodDragonBooks.com

www.ingramcontent.com/pod-product-compliance
Lightning Source LLC
Chambersburg PA
CBHW060607200326
41521CB00007B/692